Chocolate

Written by Elizabeth Ferretti

KUDOS

Published by Kudos, an imprint of Top That! Publishing plc.
Copyright © 2004 Top That! Publishing plc,
Tide Mill Way, Woodbridge, Suffolk, IP12 IAP.
www.kudosbooks.com

Kudos is a Trademark of Top That! Publishing plc

Contents

Introduction

For thousands of years chocolate has been credited with mystical powers, seen as an elixir of life and, in modern times, as a symbol of romance and mender of broken hearts.

Its history can be traced back to the ancient peoples of Central and South America. Early civilisations gave a religious significance to their beloved cocoa and their descendants still give offerings of cacao to their gods to this day.

Chocolate may even have helped change the course of history. One of the great riches of the 'New World' discovered by the Conquistadors, a vein of chocolate runs through many historical events: imperialism and the slave trade, revolutions planned in the coffee houses of 17th-century Europe, the Industrial Revolution, and as a welcome boost to the flagging morale of troops in many wars.

Today, it is impossible to imagine a world without chocolate. In the words of Milton Hershey, founder of the Hershey Chocolate Company,

> *'[c]aramels are only a fad.*
> *Chocolate is a permanent thing.'*

The Olmec and Maya, ancient peoples of Central America, believed that of all the trees in paradise, the most precious was the cacao tree.

The Food of the Gods

It was the gods who had generously revealed the secret of the cacao bean to them. The Olmec discovered a passion for the unassuming beans hidden in the fleshy fruit of the cacao tree over three thousand years ago and this set in motion the long relationship between humans and chocolate.

The more sophisticated Maya have provided us with the first real evidence of chocolate drinking in pre-Columbian America. State-of-the-art scientific techniques have revealed cocoa residues in 2,600-year-old ceramic pots, unearthed in Mayan burial sites. Cacao is described as being the food of the gods in the handful of Mayan texts which survive from that time and cacao pods appear in enigmatic carvings on the stones of their ruined buildings. To the Maya, the pods symbolised life and fertility; anthropologists have even witnessed their descendants using cacao beans in coming-of-age ceremonies and healing rituals in modern Mexico.

The Maya probably enjoyed their chocolate as a cold, frothy drink and believed it to be a health elixir. This drink was prepared by pouring the liquid from one vessel held in the air to another on the ground. Mixed in this way, the fatty 'butter' in the cacao produced a thick head of rich foam — the most highly prized part of the drink. This concoction would be unrecognisable to modern chocoholics as it was flavoured with a whole variety of spices, including chilli, but was made without sugar and was very bitter. Today, we can still find the unusual combination of chocolate and chilli in mole (a spicy Mexican chicken dish) and in chilli con carne.

5

Cacao Currency

The Maya held the cacao bean in such high esteem that it was used as a form of currency. Their complex accounting system was made up of standard measures – the zontle (the equivalent of 400 beans), the xiquipil (seven zontles) and the carga (equal to 8,000 beans). This use of 'money' helped trade develop and the Maya civilisation was born – not a bad pedigree for the humble cacao bean.

The Aztecs

The next Meso-Americans to carry on the cacao tradition were the Aztecs, whose fearsome warriors demanded tribute payments of cacao beans from defeated tribes as they created their great empire. Coming to the height of their power around 1500 AD, the Aztecs believed that wisdom, power and strength came from eating the fruit of the cacao tree. Their warriors used it to sustain them on long marches and it was said that they felt no fatigue.

Quetzalcoatl and the Chocolate Tree

The Aztecs credited their god, Quetzalcoatl – the god of civilisation representing the forces of good and light – with teaching humans how to use plants. One myth describes him coming down from the heavens on the beam of a morning star carrying 'cacahuaquahitl' (the cacao tree) which he had stolen from paradise.

The Aztecs roasted their sun-dried beans in pots, then removed the husks to obtain the cocoa-rich 'nibs'. These were then ground on a hollow, oblong stone called a 'metate'. The ground beans could be added to maize to make a sort of gruel, or porridge, called 'atolle', or mixed with water to make a drink called 'xocoatl'.

Chocolate was a high-status commodity, only available to the elite. The Aztecs probably served chocolate after a meal, in special cups (called 'xicalli') made from hollow gourds. It was flavoured with a huge variety of spices, flowers and seeds including vanilla, allspice, chilli powder and achiote – the seeds of the annatto tree which are used to this day as a natural food colorant.

Achiote gave the drink a distinctive orange-red colour reminiscent of blood. Could this be the source of the controversial link between xocoatl and the reputedly widespread Aztec practice of human sacrifice?

Columbus

Christopher Columbus was the first European to see the cacao bean. Arriving off the coast of the area that is now known as Honduras, in 1502, on his fourth and final voyage of discovery to the New World, Columbus saw an amazing sight. His son later described the scene:

'A large, local boat with 25 rowers came out to meet us. Their chief, sheltered by a roof, offered us cloth, beautiful copper objects and almonds which they use as money and from which they make a drink.'

He noticed that if one of these 'almonds' fell to the ground, one of the local people would rush to pick it up.

Not realising the significance of what he had witnessed, Columbus turned his ships south, away from the undiscovered Aztec kingdom and their precious cacao beans. It was left to the Spanish Conquistadors to understand the true potential of cacao beans some fifteen years later.

Montezuma and the Conquistadors

Montezuma, the last and most notorious of the Aztec kings, was reputed to have drunk fifty cups of the spicy xocoatl a day.

This early chocoholic based his wealth and influence on stockpiles of cacao beans which he stored in vast warehouses. Rumour had it that his consumption went up dramatically before entering his harem, though some modern scholars put this rumour down to the marketing skills of the first Spanish cacao bean traders.

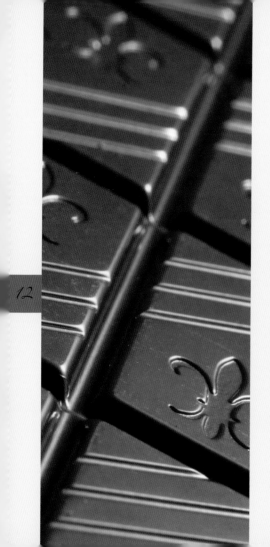

In 1519, Montezuma met his match in the canny and ruthless Hernando Cortez and the Conquistadors.

When the white-skinned and bearded Spanish arrived in the capital on horseback, the Aztecs, because of an ancient prophecy, believed them to be the descendants of Quetzalcoatl. As a sign of hospitality befitting these descendants of their god, the Aztecs served them their prized chocolate drink in beautiful golden goblets. However, within two years of Cortez' arrival, Montezuma had been murdered and the Aztec civilisation lay in ruins.

Loathsome Concoction
Most of the early European visitors were suspicious of the drink, finding it too bitter and unpalatable – presumably the Aztecs had not developed the European

'sweet tooth'. One contemporary Spanish missionary described it as:

> *'Loathsome to such as are not acquainted with it, having a scum or froth that is very unpleasant to taste.'*

To make the concoction more agreeable to Europeans, Cortez and his countrymen decided to try sweetening it with cane sugar. Neither were they satisfied with the traditional method of foaming the chocolate by pouring it from one container to another. After the Conquest, Spanish settlers developed the 'molinillo', a wooden whisk-like tool that was turned quickly between the palms of the hands to mix the chocolate and create a foam. Molinillos are still commonly found in Mexico and are similar to the modern swizzle stick. At some point it was also decided that the drink tasted a lot better if it was served hot.

Xocolata a la tassa

The Cacao Bean Reaches Europe

In his reports to the Holy Roman Emperor, Charles V, Hernando Cortez described xocoatl as a:

'drink that builds up resistance and fights fatigue,'

and emphasised its health-giving and aphrodisiac properties. He went on to say:

'[the Aztecs] value [cacao] so highly that it is treated like currency throughout their land and they buy with it everything they need, in the markets and elsewhere.'

Cortez certainly recognised its value and is said to have owned a number of cacao plantations.

Charles V was probably the first European monarch to be presented with cacao beans. It is possible that Cortez himself, returning victorious from the new Spanish colonies, arrived at court with sacks of cacao beans and all the equipment and flavourings needed to prepare chocolatl, as it was now being called. Chocolatl soon became a popular drink with the Spanish aristocracy – it was still too rare and expensive for anyone else.

For many decades the Spanish succeeded in keeping a monopoly on the production and preparation of the cacao bean. At first, this was because no-one seemed particularly interested in the beans.

Up until the late 16th century, English buccaneers were attacking Spanish galleons and destroying their precious cargoes of cocoa beans believing they were sheep droppings!

The Spanish plantations were hidden away in their inaccessible colonies in the New World and the preparation of the beans was carried out in remote monasteries far away from the eyes of their increasingly curious European neighbours.

Stories abound about how the Spanish eventually lost their exclusive hold on cocoa but it was probably the result of a gradual trickling out of information through religious networks, writings and merchants rather than by any single act of commercial espionage.

Chocolate Arrives in Europe

In 1600, Grand Duke Ferdinand of Tuscany threw the most opulent feast in the history of the kingdom to celebrate the wedding of his niece, Maria, to King Henry IV of France.

High on the list of exotic dishes and precious wines offered to guests was a milk-based drink flavoured with cocoa

and called cioccolatte. Cocoa was probably
introduced to the court in Florence by an
enterprising Italian merchant, called
Francesco Carletti, who discovered it on
one of his voyages to South America.

It is believed that chocolate arrived in
France when the fiercely Spanish princess,
Anna, married King Louis XIII in 1615.
She introduced a number of Spanish
customs to the French court, including the
drinking of chocolate which became an
instant success.

Whilst enjoying the pleasant taste of their
chocolate drink, the Europeans at this
time emphasised its health-giving
properties. One contemporary account
states that chocolate:

*'restores energy and strengthens the
stomach and brain… combats feelings of
melancholy, improves digestion and can
be used to counter the effects of wine.'*

The Great Catholic Chocolate Debate

While some doctors were praising its health benefits and the courts of Europe were showing signs of addiction, the Church was not so sure that chocolate was a good thing.

The argument centred on fasting, during Lent and on holy days, and whether the chocolate drink should be classed as food and therefore be forbidden during a fast. The debate raged through many decades and past many popes, but was mostly resolved when it was officially declared that 'Liquidum non fragit jejunum,' or 'liquids do not break the fast'. However, the more puritanical still took the view that chocolate was far too nourishing and sustaining to be allowed during religious fasting.

Death by Chocolate

The troubled relationship between the church and chocolate sometimes took a more serious turn.

One story, recounted by an English missionary living in Mexico around 1630, tells of the Bishop of Chiapas. Some of the women in his congregation had taken to having chocolate throughout church services. The Bishop complained that they had turned the church into a coffee shop and banned chocolate drinking at church. The women were furious and when, not long after, the unfortunate bishop was found dead, rumour had it that they had killed him – by putting poison in his cup of chocolate.

Officially, Pope Clement XIV died peacefully in his bed in 1774 after a short illness, but rumours soon spread that he had, in fact, been poisoned when his cup of hot chocolate was laced with arsenic. Many blamed the Jesuits, whom he had suppressed the year before and who appeared delighted by news of his death.

The English Coffee House

Chocolate drinking became all the rage in the courts and salons of Europe from 1600.

However, it only spread across the Channel to Great Britain after the 1650s when the first of the famous London coffee houses appeared. One was called 'At the Coffee Mill and Tobacco Roll' and served chocolate in the Spanish style. A recipe for making chocolate, published in 1652 from an earlier Spanish source, is as follows:

'Of Cacaos, 700, of white Sugar, one pound and a halfe, Cinnamon, 2 ounces; of long red pepper, 14, of Cloves, halfe an ounce: Three Cods of the Logwood or Campeche tree; or in steade of that, the weight of 2 Reals, or a shilling of Anniseeds; as much of Agiote (achiote), as will give it the colour, which is about the quantity of a Hasellnut. Some put in Almons, kernells of Nuts, and Orenge-flower-water."

Coffee houses quickly became fashionable and it was here that the issues and intrigues of the day were hotly debated over cups of chocolate. Samuel Pepys, the great English diarist and frequenter of coffee houses, makes a number of references to chocolate in his diaries and would seem to have been a real fan.

Cacao plantations had always been reliant on slave labour but in the later part of the 17th century the area planted with cocoa increased, and the number of mainly African slaves working on it went up dramatically. With the resulting lowered costs of production, the price of cacao beans gradually dropped, making cocoa more affordable and fuelling yet more demand.

The Development of Modern Chocolate

During the Industrial Revolution chocolate 'factories' began to appear throughout Europe but technology remained basic.

Chocolate Mill

Real developments took place in Massachusetts in the 1760s when Irishman John Hannon, a cacao bean importer, and the American Dr James Baker built the first water-powered chocolate mill. The beans were ground and pressed into cakes which were used to make drinking chocolate. The company later went on to make the famous Baker's® chocolate and was bought out by General Foods in 1927.

The Invention of Dutch Cocoa

Although some bakers in England had started to use cocoa in their products it was Dutchman Coenraad Van Houten, a chemist and chocolate manufacturer from Amsterdam, who patented a method of preparing powdered cocoa which made it much easier to use.

In 1828, Van Houten found a way of pressing the fat from roasted cacao beans. The centre of the bean, the 'nib', contains an average 54 per cent of a natural fat called cocoa butter. Van Houten's press reduced the cocoa butter content by nearly half. When alkaline salts were added to this solid it mixed more easily with water – it was the first modern cocoa powder.

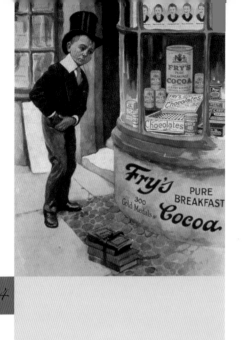

The First Bar of Chocolate

English chocolate manufacturer Joseph Fry & Son was founded in 1728. In 1847, managed by the founder's great-grandson, Fry's developed a way of mixing cacao butter, sugar and cocoa powder to create a paste that could be formed into a solid chocolate bar, thereby creating the world's first eating chocolate. The bar was called Chocolat Délicieux à Manger and, for a time, Fry's was the biggest chocolate manufacturer in the world.

Milk Chocolate

Henri Nestlé, a baby food manufacturer from Switzerland, spent eight years experimenting with ways to mix cocoa and condensed milk. Together with his associate, Daniel Peter, he succeeded in creating the first milk chocolate in 1875.

Conching

In 1879, Rodolphe Lindt of Switzerland invented a means of refining chocolate by a process of heating and rolling. The process was called 'conching' after the shell-like vats used by Lindt. The resulting high-quality fondant chocolate had a smooth, fine texture and melted in the mouth.

25

Milton Hershey

Milton Hershey, founder of the Chicago-based Lancaster Caramel Company, saw German chocolate-making machinery at the Chicago International Exposition in 1893. He bought the equipment and soon began producing his own chocolate coatings for caramels as well as making cocoa, sweet chocolate and baking chocolate.

In 1900, Hershey sold the Lancaster Caramel Company for $1 million. However, he retained the chocolate manufacturing equipment and the rights to manufacture chocolate, believing a large market existed for mass-produced chocolate confectionery. Using the money from the sale of Lancaster he set up his chocolate factory in Pennsylvania's dairy country, where he could obtain the large quantities of fresh milk needed to make milk chocolate. His highly mechanised, modern factory opened in 1905 and became what is now the world's largest chocolate manufacturing plant. Hershey's Chocolate is still the US's leading domestic producer of chocolate products.

HERSHEY'S®

MILK CHOCOLATE

27

HERSHEY'S MILK CHOCOLATE

The Business of Chocolate

Chocolate is big business and figures show that it is getting even bigger. According to the International Cocoa Organisation, the global confectionery market reached an estimated value of $73.2 billion in 2001, a 21 per cent increase since 1996.

During the second half of the 20th century, the cocoa market has been transformed into a multi-billion dollar industry, employing millions of people worldwide. The Aztecs would be astonished to see the progress their precious cocoa bean has made.

Greedy Brits

Sixty per cent of all chocolate is consumed in the USA and European Union, even though these two areas represent only twenty per cent of the world's population. The leaders on the chocolate-eating league table are the Swiss with an average consumption of over 10 kg (22 lb) per person per year, while Americans eat about 5 kg (11 lb) per person.

The British get through a whopping 550,000 tonnes of chocolate confectionery a year, or about 9 kg (20 lb) per person, spending £4 billion in the process.

Lungs of the Economy

In 1878, Tetteh Quarshie returned to his native Ghana from Equatorial Guinea with a handful of cocoa beans. These first few beans were to transform his country's economy. Cocoa, today grown by up to a million Ghanaian farmers, accounts for 45 per cent of the country's exports. In 1885, Ghana exported its first cocoa to Britain and is now the UK's main supplier.

Once the Spanish had lost their monopoly on cocoa, plantations gradually spread to the Caribbean, West Africa and Asia. As the early cocoa pioneers discovered, however, the cocoa tree requires particular growing conditions and only does well in a narrow belt around the equator. In spite of this, cocoa trees now cover over seven million hectares in West Africa, South East Asia and Latin America.

Today, millions of people in the poor cocoa-producing countries of West Africa are totally dependent on cocoa for their livelihoods. Most cocoa comes from Côte d'Ivoire (Ivory Coast) which produces over forty per cent of the world's cocoa beans, followed by Ghana and Indonesia fourteen per cent), with Nigeria, Brazil and Cameroon at around five per cent each. Between them these countries produce approximately three million tonnes of cocoa beans annually. In Côte d'Ivoire, cocoa is so important that it is described locally as being the 'Lungs of the Economy'.

32

After harvest, the fate of the cocoa beans is taken out of the hands of the farmer. Shipped off in jute bags and stored in vast, approved warehouses at major ports in Europe and America, the cocoa beans are then traded in the high-pressure world of the agricultural commodity exchanges.

As with coffee and tea, international trade in cocoa is dominated by four companies which control nearly eighty per cent of global trade and have been able to use their buying power to keep cocoa prices at record lows over the last decade.

Cocoa is an internationally traded agricultural product known as a 'soft' commodity. The three million tonnes of cocoa beans produced annually are mainly traded through the Chicago Board of Trade, the world's biggest agricultural commodity exchange, or as cocoa futures at the London futures exchange, LIFFE.

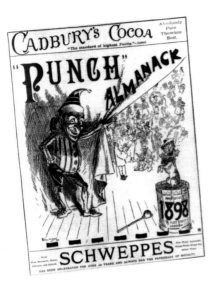

Chocolate Giants

The world market leaders in chocolate confectionery who account for a large percentage of cocoa bean use are well-known household names. The world's number one is Mars, also known as Masterfoods, with nearly sixteen per cent of the market, followed by Nestlé Rowntree (fourteen per cent), Hershey Foods Corp, (nine per cent), with Cadbury Schweppes and Kraft Suchard at around seven per cent.

Fighting it out at the top, well over £100 million a year is spent advertising chocolate in the UK alone – global spending soars to billions. Competition is tough and, with new products and brands appearing all the time, the huge advertising spend is seen as the only way to keep brands on top.

In 2001 Nestlé spent over £9 million on advertising KitKat in the UK alone. The top three chocolate confectionery brands in the UK are Cadbury's Dairy Milk, Nestlé's Quality Street, and the Mars bar. In the US the top three are M&M's, Hershey and Snickers.

Many of our best-known brands have been around a long time. Early successes were Hershey's Milk Chocolate Bar invented in 1900, Cadbury's Dairy Milk (1905), Fry's Turkish Delight (1914) and the Flake (1920). Snickers, Crunchie, KitKat, Rolos and Smarties all date from the 1930s, while M&Ms were sold from 1941.

35

Advertising the Product

The chocolate industry is worth billions of pounds each year. Companies are therefore willing to invest millions in advertising their products to maintain brand awareness and keep sales at healthy levels.

The marketing of chocolate has been so successful that most of us can recall an advertising slogan associated with one brand or another. Who is not familiar with such phrases as 'Have a break, have a KitKat', 'Do you love anyone enough to give them your last Rolo?' and, of course, 'A Mars a day helps you work, rest and play'?

We have also become familiar with campaigns, such as the ones featuring the Milky Bar Kid and the mysterious action man delivering Milk Tray 'all because the lady loves' it. Perhaps most famously of all, at least with men of a certain age, is the overtly sexual campaign featuring a pretty model relaxing in the bath while eating a Flake to the tune of 'Only the flakiest, crumbliest chocolate, tastes like chocolate never tasted before'.

'Have a break, have a KitKat' was first used by Nestlé in 1957 and proved so successful that it is still used today. The importance of advertising in the world of chocolate can be seen by the fact that the slogan itself has been the subject of legal action.

When Nestlé tried to register the words 'Have a Break' as a trademark, Mars successfully objected, leaving them free to market a bar called 'Have a Break' should they wish.

While fortunes are invested in advertising chocolate brands each year, campaigns have not always been so sophisticated. The effort to increase Milky Way's sales in the 1940s with the slogan 'Good aren't they?' may have been acceptable at the time, but a copywriter who suggested such a tagline today would be unlikely to keep their job for long.

GOOD AREN'T THEY?

No wonder Milky Way candy bars are such a favorite with the young crowd! What's more, Milky Ways are as wholesome and nourishing as they are delicious. The pure milk chocolate coating, the layer of smooth, creamy caramel and the luscious center of chocolate nougat, richly flavored with real malted milk, blend with each bite, into that delightful taste treat found only in a Milky Way.

37

Profile of a Giant

Mars, Inc, now called Masterfoods, is owned and controlled by the Mars family. This confectionery giant is one of the world's biggest private companies. Annual sales top $17 billion and it employs over thirty thousand people. Mars' rise to market dominance has been meteoric – it has grown from a turnover of $300 million at the start of the 1970s into a multi-billion dollar food empire with Mars products available in over one hundred countries worldwide.

The History of Mars

In 1911 Frank Mars and his wife, Ethel, started making and selling caramels at their home in Tacoma, Washington. According to company literature, Frank took a trip to a local drugstore in 1920 with his son, Forrest. Inspired by the malted chocolate milk drinks on sale, he came up with the idea of a solid, more portable version – the Milky Way. Forrest eventually took over the business and went on to develop the hugely successful Snickers and Mars chocolate bars.

Rumour has it, however, that the increasingly bad-tempered and paranoid Forrest Mars became obsessed with market dominance and with maintaining his fortune – even to the extent, it is said, of denying his own children chocolate treats. The company, still notoriously secretive, is now owned by three of Frank and Ethel's grandchildren and their families. Their top brands have made the Mars family one of the richest in the world. Chairman John Franklyn, together with his sister, vice-president Jacqueline, and brother, Forrest Edward Jr, are estimated to have a personal fortune totalling $10.4 billion and appear high up on Forbes' list of the four hundred richest Americans.

M&M's

It is claimed that after seeing soldiers eating sugar-coated chocolate drops in the Spanish Civil War, Forrest Mars invented M&M's, although at the time, some accused him of taking the idea from Rowntrees' Smarties. Advertised with the famous strap line 'they melt in your mouth, not in your hands', M&M's are now the world's number one confectionery brand.

M&M's got a huge marketing boost when Mars asked fans to choose a new colour. The original 1941 colours were red, yellow, green, brown, orange and violet – the choice for a new colour was between purple, aqua and blue.

This radical new tactic in the battle for market dominance resulted in over ten million Internet votes from two hundred countries. The vote placed purple at the top and gave M&M's worldwide product profile a real boost in the process.

The Mars Bar

Mars' trademark product in the UK is the Mars bar. Launched by Forrest Mars in 1933, it was the first time a manufacturer had successfully stuck chocolate to caramel. The slogan, which for forty years was associated with the Mars Bar, 'A Mars a day, helps you work, rest and play' was created in 1959 by Murray Walker, the UK's most famous motor racing commentator, while he was working as a copywriter. It is estimated that a total of sixty billion Mars bars have been sold during the last seventy years.

Hershey's

The Hershey name is little known outside the United States, but on its home territory it is the undisputed confectionery king. Some of the company's most popular products are cocoa (drinking chocolate), milk chocolate, Hershey's Kisses and Reese's Peanut Butter Cups.

The Hershey Chocolate Co, was founded in Pennsylvania, in 1903, by Milton Hershey. In contrast to the reputation of the Mars family, Hershey was a generous man who used the profits from his company to build a town for his workers to live in.

Hershey's generosity affected every aspect of town life from affordable housing, to donations to the church and the development of a public transport system, as well as the Hershey Theatre,

Hotel Hershey, and an ice hockey rink. In 1918, thirty years before his death, Hershey donated his entire estate to a trust. Now worth $5 billion, the trust supports and educates many disadvantaged children at a school Hershey established in 1909.

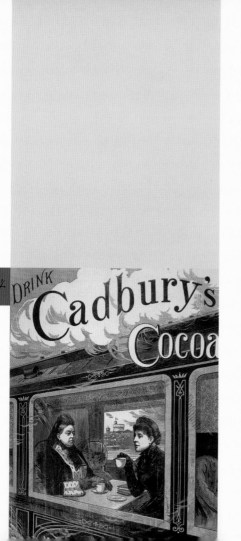

Cadbury

Cadbury is the leading confectionery manufacturer in the UK with 28 per cent of the market. Its most famous brands are Dairy Milk, Flake, Crunchie, Creme Egg, Roses and Heroes.

The Early History

Like Hershey's, Cadbury's has a strong tradition of philanthropy. John Cadbury opened a shop selling coffee and tea in Birmingham in 1824, and cocoa and drinking chocolate were introduced soon after. As a Quaker, John Cadbury believed that alcohol was one of the causes of the deprivation of working people in Britain at that time. His aim was to provide tea, coffee and cocoa as an alternative.

Cadbury was soon producing chocolate on an industrial scale and, by 1878, the business had expanded to such an extent that a new factory was needed. Richard and George Cadbury, sons of John, chose the now famous Bournville site and built one of the world's largest chocolate factories.

Bournville Village

Next to the factory, John Cadbury's sons created the first purpose-built village in Britain. They provided good, affordable housing with large gardens and open green spaces, together with working conditions that were the envy of the rest of the Victorian working class. Richard and George Cadbury had created something that was ahead of its time and the formula worked – the village of Bournville has been described as the nicest place to live in Britain.

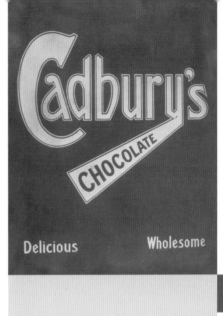

Delicious   Wholesome

46

A New Future for Chocolate?

Most of the well-known chocolate brands actually contain only a small percentage of cocoa solids with the rest of the ingredients comprising mainly sugar and fat in various forms.

The increasingly sophisticated consumer is cottoning on to this and tastes are beginning to shift away from mass-market chocolate to more expensive, better-quality varieties containing a higher percentage of cocoa solids.

In America, growth in sales of gourmet chocolate is seven times that of mainstream products, and this trend is reflected in Europe. As with many other retail sectors, the Internet is having a profound effect on the chocolate market.

Chocolates are an ideal mail order product and, through the web, even tiny specialist companies now have access to millions of people without huge marketing costs. It is a sign of the times that Amazon.com has launched a gourmet food shopping area on its US website where chocolate products feature prominently.

Many gourmet chocolate lovers are only happy with a cocoa solid percentage of seventy or above. Unusual and challenging flavours are also finding new fans, including Montezuma's favourite combination of chocolate and chilli.

The Science of Chocolate

The cacao tree grows in a specific habitat and does not adapt well to new conditions.

The Choosy Cacao Tree

It is in the rainforest belt around the equator, where the climate is moist and warm all year and where the forest provides shade and protection against the wind, that the cacao tree flourishes. To complicate matters, the cacao flower is pollinated by only one type of small fly which lives in the rainforest.

In plantation conditions the tree is susceptible to two devastating diseases, black pod disease and witches broom, as well as insect damage. In fact, worldwide production levels have decreased dramatically over recent years as a result of these problems. In the long term, the cocoa industry's Sustainable Tree Crops Programme and an increase in organic production should go some way to improving the situation.

Both aim to improve biodiversity and sustainability which should lead to healthier, more productive plants.

There are two main varieties of cacao – criollo from Central and South America, and forastero which is mainly grown in West Africa. There is also the hybrid trinitario. The criollo bean is considered superior and is reserved for producing the finest-quality chocolate, however, it accounts for only about ten per cent of cocoa production.

How is Cocoa Made?

Cacao seeds grow inside oval-shaped pods, surrounded by a sweet pulp. The yellow pods are harvested with a sharp knife or machete in May and October/November, and the sticky pulp removed from the seeds by hand. Before being taken from the rainforest, the seeds are treated to prevent rotting and then fermented in heaps for five to six days under plantain leaves. It is this process

which determines the quality and flavour of the final cocoa product.

Following fermentation, the beans are dried in the sun for up to twelve days to remove the remaining moisture. The cacao beans are then roasted and, in a process known as kibbling, broken into small pieces called nibs. These nibs are ground into cocoa mass, which contains just over fifty per cent cocoa butter. Most of this butter is removed, leaving chocolate liquor. The secret of chocolate's success lies in the fact that this liquor only starts to melt at about 38°C (100°F) which happens to be the temperature of the human tongue!

Connoisseurs look for a high percentage of cocoa solids in their chocolate, but the processing of the bean from harvest to end product also influences the quality and flavour. Look out for single estate or carefully blended brands of chocolate – the extra cost will be worth it.

What Makes Chocolate?

Sugar, cocoa butter and sometimes other vegetable fats and flavourings are added to cocoa in varying amounts to make the final chocolate product. The best will contain a higher percentage of cocoa solids and no vegetable fats. Dark, gourmet chocolate is made with cocoa solids, cocoa butter, sugar, real vanilla and sometimes soya lecithin. It should have a cocoa content of between 55 per cent and 75 per cent. Simply adding milk to this makes milk chocolate which has about 32 per cent cocoa solids.

White chocolate is made of cocoa butter, sugar and milk and contains no cocoa solids – technically it is not chocolate at all. Most commercial chocolate is produced using quite different ingredients. It usually consists of milk, vegetable fats, a lot of sugar and not much cocoa. Low-quality cocoa beans are also used which often have little flavour.

Manufacturing Chocolate

Inside a chocolate factory, precision instruments regulate temperatures, stabilise air moisture content and control the time intervals of manufacturing operations.

The cocoa beans must pass through tonnes of heavy, complex and expensive equipment on their way to becoming chocolate.

A number of fascinating machines are used to shape and package the chocolate into the familiar forms found in the shops. The shaping machines can perform at terrific speeds, squirting out jets of chocolate that solidify into special shapes at a rate of several hundred per minute. Other machines wrap and pack at speeds that human hands would find impossible. It's all a far cry from the days when thousands of workers were needed to pack sweets or assemble Easter eggs.

While the mechanisation of chocolate manufacture has meant that there are fewer jobs available on the factory floor it has also led to huge improvements in the standard of hygiene.

Two types of machines are used in the production of assorted chocolates. Some manufacturers use enrober machines which receive lines of assorted centres (nuts, nougats, etc.) and shower them with liquid chocolate. Others prefer to create a hollow, moulded chocolate shell which is then filled with a soft, or liquid, centre and then sealed with chocolate at the bottom.

Of course, when we eat a chocolate bar we do not consider the care that has been taken to bring us the taste we expect. We are barely aware of the quality tests being run in the factories but these cover a huge range. There are tests for the viscosity of chocolate, for the cocoa butter content, for acidity, for the fineness of a product and, of course, tests for purity and taste.

52

Exploding the Myths

Throughout its three thousand-year history chocolate has been considered an elixir capable of curing many ailments.

Is Chocolate Bad for You?

In the last few decades, however, chocolate has been blamed for all sorts of health problems, including obesity, acne and even depression. Therefore, when the latest scientific discoveries seemed to suggest that the Aztecs had been right all along, the big confectionery giants (who had in fact funded some of the research in the first place) were keen to advertise its benefits. Research suggested that chocolate was not fattening and may contain many beneficial substances.

However, it should be remembered that the research was of pure cocoa solids and not the fat and sugar present in large quantities in most commercial chocolate bars.

Current scientific study suggests that chocolate is not a cause of migraine, is not actually addictive nor a major cause of allergies and does not contain large quantities of caffeine.

Is Chocolate Beneficial?

To date, over three hundred chemicals have been identified in cocoa beans, including caffeine, theobromine, and phenylethylamine (a bit like amphetamine), as well as a number of minerals such as magnesium, potassium, calcium and zinc, and vitamins A1, B1, B2, D and E, all known to be beneficial when taken in appropriate quantities.

High in Antioxidants

Research seems to point to a high concentration of antioxidants, known as flavonoids, in chocolate. Indeed, there are higher levels of flavonoids in chocolate than in tea, red wine, fruit and vegetables.

Antioxidants are the body's defence against free radicals which occur naturally and as a result of illnesses, pollution, smoking and ageing, and which can damage cells in the body. Dark chocolate provides over twice the level of antioxidants of milk chocolate.

Good for the Heart

Flavonoids, part of a group of substances known as polyphenols, are also thought to have a beneficial action on heart disease because they relax some of the muscle cells in the heart.

In a study published in the *Journal of the American Medical Association*, thirteen adults aged between 55 and 64 were asked to eat chocolate every day for two weeks. The results showed a significant reduction in the participants' blood pressure. Other studies have indicated that people who eat a small amount of chocolate (one to three chocolate bars per month) actually live longer than those who don't eat any.

Good for the Soul

Chocolate also contains many chemicals known to have a positive effect on mood such as theobromine and caffeine, which stimulate the central nervous system, keeping us alert and helping fight tiredness. Other substances found in cocoa are said to have a mild antidepressant effect and may produce feelings of calm and wellbeing.

Science is now helping to prove what chocolate fans have always known – chocolate makes you feel good and does wonders for your heart.

Chocolate and Romance

There may be a provable scientific link between falling in love and eating chocolate.

La Vie en Rose

Modern imaging techniques can detect which areas of the brain are active when particular emotions are experienced and scientists have made a surprising discovery – the same area of the brain becomes active when in love and when eating chocolate. Further investigation has revealed that chocolate contains small amounts of phenylethylamine, a chemical naturally released in the brain when we fall in love.

Scientists have identified a number of other mood-changing chemicals present in small quantities in chocolate. After eating chocolate our bodies have

increased levels of serotonin, which is well known for its antidepressant effects, a whole series of natural feel-good chemicals, and a substance called anandamide, which is associated with feelings of happiness.

If you look into the history of chocolate, this latest research is simply proving what people have long known.

A connection between love and chocolate can even be found in the most unlikely sources – Culpeper's authoritative *Complete Herbal*, published in the early 1800s, lists cocoa as an aphrodisiac.

The Aztecs were convinced, and as early as 1624 Viennese monks were being urged to abstain from this 'inflamer of passions'.

The Age of Libertinism

The passion for chocolate really took off in 17th- and 18th-century France. Chocolate became all the rage at the court of King Louis XV at Versailles – it was seen both as an exotic novelty and as dangerously erotic. A little French book on food from 1702 describes chocolate as 'exciting the ardours of Venus', the goddess of love.

The most famous courtesans of the time certainly made use of the fashionable drink. According to court gossip, Louis' lover, Madame de Pompadour, drank great quantities of chocolate in order to 'warm her blood'; Countess du Barry, another courtesan, was also reputed to drink chocolate with her lovers.

France's greatest libertine, the Marquis de Sade, was very aware of the properties of the cocoa bean. It is said that at one ball, organised by the Marquis, little chocolates were served spiked with crushed Spanish fly, a small European beetle reputed to be an aphrodisiac.

21st-Century Libertines?

The age of chocolate libertinism seems to be flourishing once again. At an evening billed 'Chocolate and Sex', the respectable organisation for Italian chocolate fans, Chococlub, recently presented a collection of scenes from the *Kamasutra*… made entirely from chocolate.

Well-known names are also part of the trend. Wonderbra joined forces with gourmet chocolate makers Godiva at the launch of its 'Passion' lingerie range. The day of the launch saw two models walking down the catwalk wearing little more than replica chocolate bras made by Godiva, identical in every detail to the Wonderbra products.

A number of well-established sources also stock 'chocolate body paint' amongst their 'derma-confectionery' products.

59

Valentine's Day

Of course, the link between chocolate and romance is seen most strongly in the modern tradition of Valentine's Day gifts. Every year we spend millions of pounds on romantic chocolate gifts for our loved ones. The first heart-shaped chocolate box was sold by Richard Cadbury in 1861, but the tradition really took off at the turn of the last century when mass-produced chocolates became more affordable.

Now over thirty million heart-shaped boxes of chocolates are sold each year for Valentine's Day in the US alone. With countless specially packaged chocolate gifts available, chocolate and Valentine's Day have become inextricably linked.

Chocolate Kisses

The French gourmet and bon viveur Brillat-Savarin wrote over two hundred years ago,

'Oh fortunate chocolate, which having crossed the world through a woman's smile, finds its death in a delicious, melting kiss at her lips.'

Perugina launched their little chocolate and hazelnut Baci (meaning kisses in Italian) in time for Valentine's Day in 1922. Legend has it that Luisa Spagnoli, one of the founders of the Italian chocolate company, developed this winning combination of rich, dark chocolate and hazelnut. The rather rough shape of her chocolate is said to have reminded her of a fist.

Another of her co-founders, Giovanni Buitoni, decided the little chocolate needed a better image. He improved its shape, making it smoother and rounder, wrapped it in its characteristic, blue-spangled silver foil and gave it the name of 'Baci'.

It was in the 1930s, however, that Federico Seneca, one of the creative team at Perugina, came up with the romantic idea of wrapping a literary quotation on the theme of love around each Baci.

Hershey's Kisses are as popular in the US as Baci are in Europe. Introduced in 1907 by Milton Hershey, 'the little chocolate with the big taste' with its trademark plume at the top of the wrapper is now made at a rate of up to 33 million per day. Kisses are specially wrapped in red and silver foil for Valentine's Day.

Chocolate and Culture

No longer reserved for the elite, chocolate has become an indispensable part of most people's daily routine.

All-Day Treat

From our morning 'Coco Pops™' to our evening cup of hot cocoa, it seems that there is a chocolate product to accompany us at any time of day and for any occasion or any mood. Confectionery companies are constantly finding new ways to sell their products.

For example, in recent years the market for impulse buy snacks has become phenomenal. With a bewildering variety of chocolate 'grab bars' cleverly placed at hand height at the supermarket or petrol station checkout, chocolate temptation is never far away.

Chocolate and Biscuits

The chocolate chip cookie is as much a part of American culture as apple pie. Ruth Wakefield, an American dietitian and food lecturer, is credited with creating the much-loved biscuits.

In the 1920s Ruth and her husband bought the Toll House Inn where Ruth's desserts soon became legendary. The story goes that one day, whilst preparing her favourite chocolate biscuits, she discovered she had run out of cocoa powder. Finding a bar of chocolate in her pantry she chopped it up into pieces and added it to the mixture. What made this cookie such a hit was that the chocolate did not melt, as Ruth had expected, but remained as soft, satisfying chunks. This cookie is now America's biggest seller and there are dozens of variations to the original recipe.

In the UK, some of the most famous brands are Chocolate Digestives, Jaffa Cakes and Penguins. Original McVitie Chocolate Digestives appeared on grocer's shelves in 1925 and now,

according to company literature, over seventy million packets of Chocolate Digestives are eaten each year in the UK. In the 1940s, McVitie's also created the Jaffa Cake with its distinctive sponge base, orange centre and chocolate coating.

The Penguin, with its instantly recognisable packaging, is one of Britain's best-selling biscuits. Its famous advertising slogan 'P... P... P... Pick up a Penguin' has helped maintain the Penguin's place in the biscuit tin for over sixty years.

The After-dinner Mint

The after-dinner mint thin has been part of dinner party culture since the 1960s. The strong flavour of mint has long been prized as a way to freshen the mouth after a rich dinner and mint is thought to aid digestion. Thin, crisp chocolate and the cool taste of mint make a winning combination.

The Chocolate Calendar

Giving chocolate to friends and family on special occasions is an integral part of our social calendar.

At birthdays, at Valentine's, at Easter or simply to say thank you, chocolate in decorative boxes, or moulded into seasonal figures, has become a universal symbol of celebration.

The Easter Tradition

In the 17th century the church banned the drinking of chocolate during periods of fasting and religious contemplation, such as Lent. It was only on Easter Sunday that the dutiful faster was allowed to go back to chocolate and this may be one of the reasons why chocolate has become synonymous with Easter. Even today, it is often chocolate which Christians give up for Lent.

Each country has its own special Easter traditions, the only constant is the presence of chocolate. In northern Europe, an Easter hare hides chocolate eggs all over houses or gardens for children to find. A bell is rung to mark the start of the scramble and little baskets are given to the children to fill with as many eggs as possible.

In Italy, huge Easter eggs wrapped in brightly coloured foil fill the shop shelves and hand-decorated eggs, often works of chocolate art, can be seen in the windows of confectioners and bakers throughout the country.

In the UK, Fry's introduced their first chocolate Easter eggs in 1873 and it is still the mass-produced Easter egg from the big chocolate manufacturers, often with Disney or TV tie-ins, which has taken over our Easter. Cadbury's Creme Egg is another big Easter success. First introduced by Cadbury's in the 1920s, with its modern version available since 1971, over two hundred million are sold each year. This translates, say Cadbury's, to about three for every person in the UK.

66

Chocolate Trick or Treat?

At Hallowe'en, many little ghouls and witches will only be placated with a handful of chocolate treats, and for Americans, Thanksgiving would simply not be the same without a bowl of chocolates and other candy to share with family and friends.

Chocolate plays an important part in celebrations at Christmas. More than a hundred and fifty million chocolate Santas are made each year in the US and many families now hang chocolate treats on their Christmas trees. Boxes of chocolates are a favourite gift at any time of the year, but, in the US, more boxed chocolates are sold between Thanksgiving and New Year's Day than at any other time.

The Art of Chocolate

Chocolate has also become a feature of the world of art and literature. Many great writers and composers are known to have been passionate about chocolate. In Mozart's comic opera, *Cosi Fan Tutte*, the maid, Despina, is shown making chocolate for her mistress. The great German Romantic, Goethe, would not travel anywhere without a personal supply. Indeed the list of famous chocoholics is endless.

In the vibrant Paris of the early 1900s, artists created mini advertising masterpieces for the chocolate makers of the time. The most famous posters are by Alphonse Mucha, whose unashamedly sentimental depiction of children was the brand image of the day. Other artists working for Poulain, Suchard and Menier include Steinlen, the creator of the *Tournée du Chat Noir* poster, and even Gustav Klimt, most famous for his golden, mosaic paintings such as *The Kiss*.

Books and Films with Chocolate Themes

Millions of children, and adults, have been enchanted by Roald Dahl's classic story, *Charlie and the Chocolate Factory*, since its publication in 1964.

The book tells the story of poor, starving Charlie Bucket who lives in one room with his parents and four bedridden grandparents. Nearby is the enormous factory owned by Willy Wonka whose genius with chocolate finds expression in his bizarre, but magical, chocolate factory. Charlie realises every child's dream when he wins one of five golden tickets giving him an exclusive tour of the factory.

He is thrown into a series of adventures with the four other delightfully horrid winners who, through their greed, all come to a sticky end. In the end it is good, unspoilt Charlie who wins the prize to beat all prizes. A musical film version was released in 1971, called *Willy Wonka And The Chocolate Factory*, starring Gene Wilder as Wonka.

The past few years have seen the appearance of a few notable books and films whose central theme is chocolate. They have enjoyed huge success with a public captivated by their heady mix of chocolate and romance.

Chocolat, by Joanne Harris, tells the story of a mysterious stranger, Vianne, who appears one day accompanied by her daughter, Anouk, to warm the cold hearts of a sleepy French village.

Pleasure does not play a part in the lives of the people until Vianne opens her chocolate shop, setting off a quiet but unstoppable revolution in the village. With exotic ingredients and secret recipes from ancient and mysterious sources, these sublime chocolates gradually win over the suspicious villagers.

The power of Vianne's creations is magical in its ability to transform lives, bringing colour, life and romance back into the

villagers' humdrum existence. The film version, directed by Lasse Hallstrom and starring Juliette Binoche and Johnny Depp, was always destined for success with its irresistible combination of stunning chocolate and romance.

Like Water for Chocolate: A Novel in Monthly Installments, with Recipes, Romances, and Home Remedies by Laura Esquivel is another bestseller with its film version a box-office hit. Like *Chocolat*, this story explores the mystical powers of love and food.

Tita is doomed to spend the best years of her life at the beck and call of her tyrannical mother. Following Mexican tradition, she must remain a spinster while her mother is alive. Unable to show her feelings or be with the man she loves, her passionate nature finds increasing outlet in food. Mexican cuisine is woven like a thread through the story and forms a delicious backdrop to this culinary romance.

Centres of Chocolate Excellence

Most major European and American cities have famous chocolate shops and cafés, but there are a number of destinations which should form part of any chocolate pilgrimage.

Hershey, Pennsylvania

In the US, chocolate heaven comes in the form of Hershey, Pennsylvania, where you can stroll along avenues called Chocolate or Cocoa, or down streets named after the cocoa-growing areas of Bahia or Caracas.

The street lights are shaped like Hershey's Kisses and the air carries the sweet smell of chocolate. There is a large museum dedicated to chocolate and a shopping mall packed with enough boutiques to satisfy even the most dedicated chocolate fan.

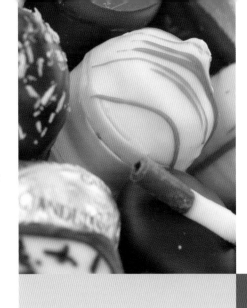

Paris

In Paris, specialist companies offer chocolate tours of the most famous master chocolate makers, as well as revealing the best-kept secrets of the French capital's sophisticated chocolate tradition.

The French academy of chocolate, called the 'Croqueurs de Chocolat' – the chocolate crunchers – was formed in 1981 by a group of serious amateurs who wanted to promote high standards in French chocolate making.

The members of this exclusive club have tasted over seven hundred chocolate products in the last twenty years. The results of all this hard work are published in the *Guide des Croqueurs de Chocolat*, where each chocolate maker worthy of inclusion is rated with up to five chocolate bars.

74

Brussels

Neuhaus, the birthplace of Belgian chocolate, was opened in the city centre by Swiss confectioner, Jean Neuhaus, in 1857. The interior of the shop has remained almost unchanged to this day with a dazzling selection of chocolates.

Mary Chocolatier on the Rue Royale is the queen of the Brussels chocolate makers. The company supplies the Belgian royal family and even President George W Bush, who tasted some of their range of seventy different pralines when he visited the country.

Pierre Marcolini, on the Place du Grand Sablon, is a world champion chocolate maker and Martine Jamart's hand-made pralines, Avenue Rommelaere, are not to be missed.

Another prize-winner is the Chocolaterie Manon, Rue du Congrès. For more unusual chocolates try Frank Duval's innovative Planete Chocolat on the Rue du Midi. If that is not enough, there is also a museum dedicated to chocolate on the main square.

Turin

The city of Turin in northern Italy has a rich tradition of chocolate making. It is the home of the gianduja chocolate, made with the best hazelnuts from Piedmont.

The town centre is dotted with excellent chocolate shops specialising in hand-made gianduja chocolates and artisan ice-cream makers selling intensely flavoured chocolate ice-cream. On a cold day, try the hot chocolate at the 'Caffè San Carlo' or the 'Caffè Torino' in Piazza San Carlo.

Truffles

Method

1. Gently heat the cream and vanilla in a heavy-based saucepan, bringing the mixture to the boil.

2. Strain the cream to remove the vanilla, then add the butter and put back on the heat, stirring occasionally until the butter has melted. Remove the mixture from the heat as soon as it comes back to the boil.

3. Add the chocolate and stir until the ingredients are well mixed.

4. Add the brandy, whisky or liqueur and whisk the mixture for two minutes. Allow the mixture to stand until cool, then refrigerate it overnight.

5. Take a small quantity of the mixture and roll it between the palms of your hands to form a neat ball shape. Repeat until you've made all the truffles.

6. Decorate each truffle with the covering of your choice. The white chocolate, if used, should be melted in a heatproof bowl over a saucepan of hot water. Allow it to cool for a few minutes, then dip some truffles in the melted chocolate, lifting each one out carefully with a fork, shaking off any excess chocolate.

Ingredients

300 ml/10 fl. oz double cream

1 vanilla pod, split down the middle

50 g/1¾ oz unsalted butter, cut into small dice

300 g/10 oz dark chocolate, roughly chopped

40 ml/1½ fl. oz brandy, whisky or your favourite liqueur

finely grated milk chocolate, finely chopped mixed nuts or 75 g/2½ oz white chocolate (broken into pieces) to decorate

MAKES 30–35 truffles

7. After decoration, place each truffle on baking parchment, allow them to cool completely, then refrigerate before serving.

Ingredients

50 g/1¾ oz sultanas

50 g/1¾ oz Italian candied citrus peel, very finely chopped

50 ml/1¾ fl. oz brandy

150 g/5¼ oz dark chocolate

50 g/1¾ oz butter

50 g/1¾ oz ground almonds

50 g/1¾ oz chopped hazelnuts

50 g/1¾ oz dark glacé cherries, finely chopped

cocoa powder, chopped nuts and finely grated white chocolate, to decorate

MAKES 20

Method

1. Soak the sultanas and candied peel in the brandy for a few hours, stirring occasionally.

2. Melt the chocolate and butter in a heatproof bowl over a pan of gently simmering water, stirring occasionally.

3. Off the heat, add the ground almonds and allow the mixture to cool for ten minutes.

4. Add the soaked fruit, hazelnuts and glacé cherries. Leave the mixture to cool until it begins to stiffen.

5. Form the mixture into small balls, rolling each one in the cocoa powder, chopped nuts or grated chocolate. Place the fruit bites in decorative petits fours cases to serve.

Chocolate Fruit Bites

Chocolate Fruit and Nuts

Method

1. Wash and thoroughly dry the fruit, cutting it into bite-sized pieces where necessary.

2. Place the chocolate, butter and vanilla extract in a heatproof bowl over a saucepan of barely simmering water. (It is important that the bowl does not come into contact with the water.) Stir the mixture occasionally until it has just melted.

3. Take the mixture off the heat and allow it to cool for a few minutes.

4. Dip each piece of fruit into the chocolate, then place them on sheets of baking parchment.

5. Add the nuts to the remaining melted chocolate, lift them out on a fork to remove any excess chocolate and place them on baking parchment.

6. Refrigerate for 20–30 minutes prior to serving.

Ingredients

selection of fresh fruit (e.g. strawberries, raspberries, cherries, banana slices, pineapple pieces)

hazelnuts, brazil nuts and almonds

150 g/5¼ oz of dark chocolate, broken into pieces

25 g/¾ oz unsalted butter, cut into dice

1 tsp vanilla extract

MAKES 20

Ingredients

150 ml/5 fl. oz milk

150 ml/5 fl. oz single cream

100 g/3½ oz unsalted butter,
cut into small dice

400 g/14 oz white sugar

300 g/10 oz soft brown sugar

75 g/2½ oz dark chocolate,
broken into pieces

75 g/2½ oz white chocolate,
broken into pieces

Sugar thermometer

MAKES 40–50 pieces

Method

1. Line a 20 cm/8 in. square baking tin with lightly greased tin foil.

2. Place the milk, cream, butter and both types of sugar in a heavy-based saucepan. Heat them gently, stirring occasionally, until the butter has melted and the sugar dissolved. Allow the mixture to come to the boil.

3. Boil for about fifteen minutes, stirring occasionally with a wooden spoon. (At this stage the sugar thermometer should be reading 115–116°C/239–241°F.)

4. Melt the dark and white chocolate in two separate bowls over pans of hot water.

5. Divide the creamy fudge mixture equally between the two bowls of chocolate. Beat the contents of each bowl with a metal spoon until the fudge starts to become glossy.

6. Transfer the white chocolate fudge to the baking tray and smooth it with a warm palette knife. Place the dark chocolate fudge mixture on top and smooth it down.

7. Once set, the fudge can be cut into squares using a warm, sharp knife.

Creamy Double-layer Chocolate Fudge

Pears in Chocolate Sauce

Method

1. Peel the pears, leaving the stalks. Cut out the cores from the bases using a sharp knife.

2. Gently heat the wine, sugar and lemon zest and bring to the boil.

3. Stand the pears in the saucepan and cover with a close-fitting lid so that the pears cook in the steam.

4. Turn down the heat a little until the mixture is just boiling. Cook for 20–30 minutes, or until a knife inserts easily into a pear (the riper the fruit, the shorter the cooking time).

5. Remove the pears from the liquid and allow them to cool. Reduce the remaining liquid by boiling it rapidly in an uncovered saucepan, until it resembles a thick syrup.

6. Place the chocolate and cream in a heatproof bowl over a saucepan of barely simmering water. Stir occasionally until melted.

7. Add the wine syrup and whisk it into the chocolate mixture for two minutes. Allow it to cool, then pour it over the

Ingredients

10–12 small ripe pears
250 ml/8^{1}/$_{2}$ fl. oz fruity red wine
50 g/1^{3}/$_{4}$ oz sugar
grated zest of 1 lemon (unwaxed)
150 g/5^{1}/$_{4}$ oz dark chocolate
50 ml/1^{3}/$_{4}$ oz single cream
whipped cream to serve (optional)

SERVES 5-6

pears as it's beginning to thicken. Serve with a generous helping of freshly whipped cream.

Ingredients

200 g/7 oz dark chocolate,
minimum 70% cocoa solids,
broken into pieces

30 ml/1 fl. oz milk

1 tsp dark-roast coffee granules

5 very fresh free-range eggs,
separated

pinch of salt

SERVES 4

Method

1. Put the chocolate and the milk in a heatproof bowl over a saucepan of barely simmering water. Stir them occasionally.

2. As soon as the chocolate pieces have melted, stir in the coffee granules and immediately remove the pan from the heat.

3. Allow the mixture to cool completely, then stir in the beaten egg yolks.

4. In a clean bowl, beat the egg whites with the salt until they form stiff peaks.

5. Gradually and carefully fold the beaten egg whites into the chocolate mixture, a spoonful at a time. Continue until all the egg whites have been used.

6. Spoon the mousse into attractive glasses and refrigerate it for three hours. Before serving, sprinkle each mousse with grated dark chocolate.

Chocolate Mousse

Chocolate and Ginger Cheesecake

Method

1. Grease a 20 cm/8in. loose-bottomed springform tin with melted butter and line the base with greaseproof paper. Place the biscuits in a strong plastic food bag and crush them into fine crumbs with a rolling pin.

2. Melt the butter, then add the biscuit crumbs and cocoa powder. Stir well.

3. Press the biscuit mixture firmly into the base of the loose-bottomed tin.

4. Beat together the mascarpone, milk, icing sugar and half a tablespoon of ginger syrup. Then stir in the finely grated chocolate.

5. Spoon the mixture onto the biscuit base and refrigerate it for at least one hour.

6. To serve, remove the cheesecake from the tin and decorate it with a few thinly sliced pieces of crystallised ginger.

Ingredients

200 g/7 oz ginger biscuits
75 g/2$^{1}/_{2}$ oz unsalted butter
25 g/$^{3}/_{4}$ oz cocoa powder
600 g/1 lb 5 oz mascarpone
1 tbsp cold milk
40 g/1$^{1}/_{4}$ oz icing sugar, sifted
crystallised stem ginger in syrup
75 g/2$^{1}/_{2}$ oz dark chocolate,
finely grated

SERVES 6–8

Ingredients

1 Victoria sponge
50 ml/1¾ fl. oz brandy, whisky
or a favourite liqueur
4 egg whites
100 g/3½ oz icing sugar
dark chocolate ice cream
white chocolate ice cream

SERVES 6–8

Method

1. Preheat the oven to 230°C/450°F/ gas mark 6 and line a flat baking sheet with baking parchment.

2. Place the sponge on top and drizzle it with the brandy, whisky or liqueur.

3. In a clean bowl, beat the egg whites with half the sugar until stiff peaks are formed.

4. Fold in the remaining icing sugar, and beat the mixture until it is stiff and glossy.

5. Working quickly, place a layer of dark chocolate ice cream on the sponge and a layer of white ice cream on top.

6. Cover the ice cream and cake with the meringue.

7. Flash bake the dessert in the top of a hot oven for three to four minutes, then transfer it to a serving plate and serve immediately.

Hot Chocolate Ice Cream

Sicilian Cassata

Method

1. Cut the sponge into thin, flat slices. Use them to line a large pudding basin, keeping a few to one side.

2. Drizzle the brandy evenly over the sponge pieces.

3. Beat the ricotta with the milk until smooth. Then mix in the sugar, candied fruit and roughly grated dark chocolate.

4. Pour the ricotta mixture into the basin and finish with a layer of cake.

5. Place a plate and heavy weight on top of the basin and refrigerate it for four to five hours.

To decorate

6. Melt the broken chocolate pieces and butter in a bowl over a saucepan of hot water. Stir well, then allow the mixture to cool until it begins to thicken.

7. Turn the cassata out onto a decorative plate and drizzle over the melted chocolate mixture. Put it back in the fridge for at least one hour. Finish with pieces of candied fruit if desired. Serve very cold.

Ingredients

1 Victoria sponge

50 ml/1¾ fl. oz brandy

500 g/17½ oz ricotta

30 ml/1 fl. oz milk

200 g/7 oz caster sugar

200 g/7 oz Italian candied citrus peel, finely chopped

100 g/3½ oz dark chocolate, roughly grated

100 g/3½ oz dark chocolate, broken into pieces

25 g/¾ oz butter

SERVES 6

93

Ingredients

4 free-range eggs, separated

60 ml/2 fl. oz amaretto liqueur

100 g/3$\frac{1}{2}$ oz icing sugar, sifted

50 g/1$\frac{3}{4}$ oz cocoa powder, sifted

30 ml/1 fl. oz milk

500 g/1 lb mascarpone

100 g/3$\frac{1}{2}$ oz grated chocolate, white or dark

pinch of cream of tartar

150 g/5 oz boudoir biscuits (sponge fingers)

140 ml/5 fl. oz of very strong black coffee, cooled

SERVES 6–8

Method

1. Beat the egg yolks and amaretto until creamy. Add the sifted icing sugar, cocoa powder, milk and mascarpone and mix until smooth. Add the grated chocolate.

2. Beat the egg whites with a pinch of cream of tartar in a clean bowl until they form stiff peaks.

3. Gradually fold the beaten egg whites into the cream mixture, one spoon at a time.

4. Dip the biscuits into the coffee one at a time, arranging each one in a serving dish after dipping. Using half the biscuits, form a single layer at the bottom of the dish. Cover this layer with half the cream mixture.

5. Add another layer of coffee-dipped biscuits, finishing with a layer of cream.

6. Refrigerate for 4–5 hours. Remove the tiramisu from the fridge 30 minutes before serving and decorate it with grated chocolate.

Creamy Chocolate Tiramisu

Chocolate and Pear Double-layer Cake

Method

1. Preheat the oven to 180°C/350°F/ gas mark 4 and grease and flour a 23 cm/9 in. springform cake tin.

2. Cream together the butter and sugar until light and fluffy. Add the beaten eggs one at a time, mixing well after each one has been added.

3. Sift the flour and cocoa powder together twice. Gradually fold the flour and cocoa into the creamed mixture, a few spoonfuls at a time.

4. Transfer half the mixture to the tin and arrange a layer of pear slices over the top.

5. Mix the muscovado sugar and cinnamon, breaking up any lumps in the sugar, and sprinkle the pears with half of this. Spoon on the rest of the cake mixture and level it with a warm palette knife.

6. Place the remaining pears on top of the cake and sprinkle them with the sugar and cinnamon, and a handful of pine nuts.

7. Bake in the centre of the oven for 45–50 minutes.

Ingredients

175 g/6 oz unsalted butter, softened

150 g/5¼ oz light soft brown sugar

3 free-range eggs
(at room temperature)

175 g/6 oz self-raising flour

50 g/1¾ oz cocoa powder

3–4 ripe pears, peeled,
cored and sliced

40 g/1½ oz light muscovado sugar

1 tsp cinnamon

handful of pine nuts

SERVES 8–10

Ingredients

175 g/6 oz butter, softened
150 g/5¼ oz soft brown sugar
3 free-range eggs
(at room temperature)
1 medium courgette, finely grated
50 g/1¾ oz chocolate chips
50 g/1¾ oz marzipan,
finely chopped
175 g/6 oz self-raising flour
50 g/1¾ oz unsweetened
cocoa powder

SERVES 8

Method

1. Preheat the oven to 180°C/350°F/ gas mark 4 and grease and flour a loaf tin.

2. Cream the butter and sugar together until fluffy and pale.

3. Add the beaten eggs, one at a time. Mix well.

4. Now add the grated courgette, chocolate chips and chopped marzipan, and mix.

5. Sift together the flour and cocoa powder twice, and fold into the mixture.

6. Transfer the mixture to the loaf tin and bake for 50–55 minutes or until firm to touch.

7. Allow the loaf to cool for 15 minutes, then serve warm.

Chocolate Chip and Courgette Loaf

White Chocolate and Lime Celebration Cake

Method

1. Preheat the oven to 160°C/325°F/ gas mark 3 and grease and line a deep 25 cm/10 in. cake tin with a removable base.

2. Cream the butter and sugar together until pale and fluffy. Add the beaten eggs one at a time, mixing well, then add the sour cream and amaretto.

3. Sift the flour, cocoa powder, ground almonds, baking powder and bicarbonate of soda twice, holding the sieve up high to allow as much air into the ingredients as possible. Fold them into the cake mixture gently.

4. Transfer the mixture to the cake tin and bake for about 90 minutes. Allow the cake to cool in the tin for ten minutes, then transfer it to a cooling rack. Once cool, cut it into three or four layers using a warmed knife.

For the filling

5. Place all the ingredients for the mascarpone cream filling in a bowl and mix well. Refrigerate for 30 minutes before using.

6. Spread the filling onto the bottom layer of the cake and place the next layer on top. Continue, spreading the mascarpone cream between each layer.

7. Decorate the top and sides of the cake with the remaining cream and finish with curls or shavings of white and dark chocolate. Serve with single cream.

Ingredients

250 g/9 oz unsalted butter
400 g/14 oz caster sugar
5 free-range eggs
150 ml/5 fl. oz sour cream
1 dessertspoon amaretto almond liqueur
300 g/10 oz plain flour
100 g/$3^{1}/_{2}$ oz unsweetened cocoa powder
50 g/$1^{3}/_{4}$ oz ground almonds
1 tsp baking powder
$^{1}/_{2}$ tsp bicarbonate of soda
white and dark chocolate to decorate

For the filling:
600 g/1 lb 5 oz mascarpone
50 ml/$1^{3}/_{4}$ fl. oz milk
175 g/$7^{3}/_{4}$ oz sifted, icing sugar
grated zest and juice of two limes
75 g/$2^{1}/_{2}$ oz white chocolate, grated

SERVES 14–16

Ingredients

200 g/7 oz self-raising flour

100 g/3½ oz caster sugar

2 tsp dried coffee granules

2 free-range eggs

1 tbsp extra virgin olive oil

150 ml/5¼ fl. oz full cream milk

100 g/3½ oz white chocolate,
broken into small chunks

100 g/3½ oz fresh or
frozen mixed forest berries

1 grated dessert apple

MAKES 9 muffins

Method

1. Preheat the oven to 200°C/400°F/ gas mark 5 and grease a muffin tray, unless you are going to use muffin cases.

2. Sift the flour into the sugar and coffee granules in a large mixing bowl, leaving a well in the middle.

3. In a separate bowl, beat together the eggs, oil and milk.

4. Add the egg mixture to the flour and mix it roughly, ignoring any lumps. Then, add the white chocolate chunks, berries and apple.

5. Mix all the ingredients together roughly. Do not over-mix. Spoon immediately into the muffin tins or muffin cases, so that they are two thirds full.

6. Cook in the centre of the oven for 20–25 minutes. Allow the muffins to cool for five minutes before removing them from the tin.

7. Muffins are best enjoyed warm. Any leftover muffins can be reheated for a few minutes in the oven the next day.

Berry and White Chocolate Teatime Muffins

Simple Chocolate Cake with Chocolate Mascarpone Cream and Raspberries

Method

1. Preheat the oven to 180°C/350°F/ gas mark 4 and grease a 23 cm/9 in. springform cake tin.

2. Cream together the butter and sugar and add the beaten eggs separately. Sift the flour and cocoa together and fold them into the egg mixture. Add a teaspoonful of vanilla essence and the milk.

3. Transfer to the cake tin and bake in the centre of the oven for 35–40 minutes. Allow the cake to cool on a wire cooling rack.

For the filling

4. Beat the mascarpone and milk to form a smooth cream.

5. Melt the chocolate in a heatproof bowl over a saucepan of barely simmering water. Allow the chocolate to cool a little and then add it to the mascarpone. Add sifted icing sugar and mix well. Refrigerate for 30 minutes.

6. Cut the cake in half and spread one-third of the chocolate mascarpone on one side. Place half the raspberries on the filling and carefully replace the top half of the cake.

7. Use the rest of the mascarpone cream to decorate the top and sides of the cake. Finish with the remaining raspberries.

Ingredients

200 g/7 oz butter
150 g/5¼ oz sugar
3 free-range eggs
175 g/6 oz self-raising flour
75 g/2½ oz unsweetened cocoa powder
1 tsp vanilla essence
1 tbsp milk

For the filling:
500 g/1 lb mascarpone
15 ml/½ fl. oz milk
200 g/7 oz melted chocolate
150 g/5¼ oz sifted icing sugar
150 g/5¼ oz raspberries

SERVES 8-10

Ingredients

200 g/7 oz digestive style biscuits
150 g/5¼ oz dark chocolate
100 g/3½ oz milk chocolate
50 g/1¾ oz unsalted butter
50 g/1¾ oz honey
pinch of cinnamon
pinch of white pepper
25 g/¾ oz blanched almonds,
roughly chopped
50 g/1¾ oz candied citrus peel,
finely chopped

SERVES 8–10

Method

1. Place the biscuits in a strong plastic food bag and crush them roughly with a rolling pin.

2. Break the chocolate into small pieces and melt it in a heatproof bowl over a saucepan of simmering water, stirring occasionally. (Make sure that the bowl is not touching the water.)

3. As soon as the chocolate has melted, add the butter, cut into small dice, honey, cinnamon and pepper. Stir over the heat until well mixed. Off the heat, add the biscuits, almonds and chopped citrus peel and mix thoroughly.

4. Press into an 20 cm/8 in. greased and lined square tin and allow to cool.

5. Chill in the fridge overnight.

6. While still in the tin, cut the fridge cake into thick fingers. (They are best stored in a container in the fridge.)

7. Remove the cake from the fridge fifteen minutes before serving and sprinkle each slice with a little icing sugar.

Chocolate and Almond Fridge Cake

Double Chocolate Orange Cookies

Method

1. Preheat the oven to 180°C/350°F/ gas mark 4 and line two baking trays with baking parchment.

2. Beat the butter and sugar together until pale and fluffy.

3. Sift the flour, cocoa and baking powder together twice and then carefully fold them into the butter and sugar mixture.

4. Add the chopped chocolate, orange zest and orange juice and gently mix them together to form a smooth dough.

5. On a lightly-floured surface, roll out the dough to a thickness of 0.5 cm/ 1/4 in. Cut it into approximately 30 biscuits with a 5 cm/2 in. biscuit cutter.

6. Cook in the centre of the oven for 12–15 minutes.

7. Allow the biscuits to cool for five minutes before transferring them to a cooling rack. Store them in an airtight container when cold.

Ingredients

150 g/5¼ oz unsalted butter, softened

50 g/1¾ oz light brown sugar

225 g/8 oz plain flour

50 g/1¾ oz unsweetened cocoa powder

2 tsp baking powder

75 g/2½ oz dark chocolate, chopped

grated zest of 2 oranges

2 tbsp orange juice

MAKES about 30 cookies

Ingredients

125 g/4¹/₂ oz unsalted butter, softened
50 g/1¹/₂ oz smooth peanut butter
75 g/2¹/₂ oz sugar
2 large free-range eggs
1 tsp vanilla essence
200 g/7 oz plain flour
1 tsp baking powder
75 g/2¹/₂ oz dark chocolate, chopped
50 g/1¹/₂ oz unsalted peanuts

MAKES about 18 cookies

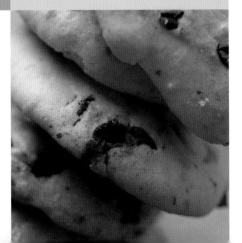

Method

1. Preheat the oven to 180°C/350°F/ gas mark 4 and line a baking tray with baking parchment.

2. Beat together the butter, peanut butter and sugar until fluffy.

3. Add the beaten eggs and vanilla essence, and mix well.

4. Sift the flour and baking powder together twice and fold them into the mixture.

5. Add the chunks of chopped dark chocolate and the peanuts. Mix in 1–2 tablespoonfuls of milk if the dough appears too stiff.

6. Place evenly spaced spoonfuls of the mixture onto the baking tray, pressing each one down with the back of a spoon. (Dipping the spoon into water will stop it sticking to the dough.)

7. Place the cookies in the centre of the oven for 20 minutes. Allow them to cool before serving.

Chocolate and Peanut Butter Cookies

Baci di Dama

Method

1. Preheat the oven to 150°C/300°F/ gas mark 2 and line two baking trays with lightly greased baking parchment.

2. In a large bowl, mix together the flour, ground almonds and sugar. Then rub in the butter to form an even crumb.

3. Add the vanilla essence and sufficient water to just bind the ingredients, forming a stiff dough. Work the dough lightly for two to three minutes.

4. Using the palms of your hands, form small amounts of dough into balls the size of cherries (there will be about 40). Place them on a baking tray and flatten each one slightly.

5. Cook them in the centre of the oven for 15–20 minutes until just golden brown and then allow them to cool on a wire rack.

For the filling

6. Place a heatproof bowl over a bowl of gently simmering water and add the chopped chocolate. Heat until the chocolate has just melted, stirring occasionally. Be careful not to overheat.

Ingredients

150 g/5¼ oz plain flour
150 g/5¼ oz ground almonds
150 g/5¼ oz caster sugar
125 g/4½ oz unsalted butter
1 tsp vanilla essence
2–3 tsp water

For the filling:
200 g/7 oz dark chocolate, chopped

MAKES 20 finished biscuits

7. Allow the chocolate to cool a little then, using a teaspoon, place a little of the melted chocolate onto the base of one of the biscuits. Take another of the biscuits and press them together. Continue until all the biscuits have been used up.

8. Allow the chocolate to cool completely before serving these delicious ladies' kisses.

Ingredients

60 ml/2 fl. oz milk
75 g/2¹/₂ oz unsalted butter
100 g/3¹/₂ oz icing sugar
50 g/1³/₄ oz plain flour
50 g/1³/₄ oz chopped nuts
50 g/1³/₄ oz flaked almonds
50 g/1³/₄ oz finely chopped
dark glacé cherries

For the chocolate coating:
100 g/3¹/₂ oz dark chocolate
10 g/¹/₃ oz unsalted butter

MAKES about 20 small florentines

Method

1. Preheat the oven to 190°C/375°F/ gas mark 4 and line two baking trays with lightly greased baking parchment.

2. In a saucepan, heat the milk, butter and sugar, stirring until the sugar has dissolved.

3. Off the heat, add the flour, chopped nuts, flaked almonds and glacé cherries. Allow the mixture to go cold, then spoon small quantities onto the baking sheets. Allow plenty of space between them as the mixture spreads when it is cooking.

4. Cook for about 7–10 minutes until golden brown. Leave to cool for ten minutes, then carefully transfer to a wire cooling rack.

For the chocolate coating

5. Melt the chocolate and butter in a heatproof bowl over a saucepan of hot water.

6. Coat the base of each florentine with a little of the chocolate mixture.

7. Allow them to cool completely, chocolate side up.

Florentines

White Chocolate and Exotic Fruit Cookies

Method

1. Preheat the oven to 190°C/375°F/ gas mark 5 and line two baking trays with lightly greased baking parchment.

2. Sift together the flour and baking powder.

3. Rub the butter into the flour with your finger tips. Add the sugar, chopped chocolate and dried fruit. Mix well.

4. Add the vanilla essence and egg, adding a little extra water if necessary, to form a soft dough.

5. Place spoonfuls of the mixture on the baking tray, pressing each cookie down slightly with the back of a spoon.

6. Cook them for 10–12 minutes until a light golden brown.

7. Allow the cookies to cool for five minutes then transfer them to a cooling rack.

Ingredients

200 g/7 oz plain flour
1 tsp baking powder
100 g/3½ oz unsalted butter
125 g/4½ oz light brown sugar
75 g/2½ oz white chocolate chopped
75 g/2½ oz of mixed exotic dried fruit such as papaya or mango, chopped
1 tsp vanilla essence
1 free-range egg

MAKES about 18 cookies

117

Classic Hot Chocolate

Method

1. Gently heat the milk with the vanilla pod.

2. Add the chocolate pieces.

3. Bring the mixture to the boil, stirring frequently.

4. Remove the vanilla pod and serve.

Ingredients

500 ml/17 fl. oz full cream milk

1 vanilla pod

250 g/9 oz chocolate
broken into pieces

SERVES 2

Ingredients

150 g/5¼ oz dark chocolate,
broken into pieces
500 ml/17 fl. oz full cream milk
1–2 egg yolks
50 ml/1¾ fl. oz of whipped cream
grated chocolate to serve

SERVES 2

Method

1. Melt the chocolate in a small amount of water in a saucepan.

2. Add the milk and gently heat for a few minutes.

3. Take the mixture off the heat and allow it to cool.

4. Beat in the egg yolk/s.

5. Reheat the mixture for two minutes, being careful not to let it boil, stirring continuously.

6. Off the heat, strain the mixture, whisk it into a froth and serve.

7. Finish with a generous helping of whipped cream and some finely grated chocolate.

Viennese Hot Chocolate

Xocoatl

Method

1. Gently heat the milk with the vanilla, cinnamon stick and chilli powder for one minute.

2. Add the chocolate and mix until completely melted.

3. Off the heat, allow the ingredients to infuse for 5–10 minutes.

4. Strain the mixture to remove the vanilla and cinnamon, then gently reheat it, being careful not to let it boil.

5. Add honey to taste.

6. Whisk and serve topped with whipped cream and grated chocolate.

Ingredients

500 ml/17 fl. oz full cream milk

1 vanilla pod, split in half

1 cinnamon stick

a small pinch of chilli powder

150 g/5$^{1/4}$ oz dark chocolate, grated or chopped

honey

whipped cream

grated chocolate to serve

SERVES 2

Ingredients

100 g/3$^1/_2$ oz dark chocolate
50 g/1$^3/_4$ oz sugar
a large cup of strong black espresso
a dash of rum
whipped cream

SERVES 1–2

Method

1. Gently heat the chocolate, sugar and espresso with some water to taste.

2. Mix until completely dissolved.

3. Off the heat, add a dash of rum.

4. Serve in warmed cups and top with the cream.

Chocolate Shock

Montezuma

Method

1. Place a heatproof bowl above a pan of simmering water, making sure that it does not touch the water.

2. Heat the milk and chocolate in the bowl, stirring frequently until the chocolate has melted.

3. Mix it well and allow the mixture to cool.

4. Once cool, place the mixture in the fridge for about an hour.

5. Put the honey, lemon zest, rum, gin, chilli and ginger in a liquidiser.

6. Liquidise them for a few seconds, then strain.

7. Add the liquid to the cold milk and chocolate mixture.

8. Shake it together vigorously in a cocktail shaker and serve.

Ingredients

350 ml/17 fl. oz milk
100 g/3^1/$_2$ oz dark chocolate
^{1}/$_2$ tbsp of honey
grated zest of half a lemon (unwaxed)
1 measure of rum
^{1}/$_2$ measure of gin
pinch chilli powder
pinch ground ginger

SERVES 2

Conclusion

128

The cocoa used for these products is grown using traditional methods, on small farm holdings deep in the rainforest without a plantation or pesticide in sight, in the lands of the ancient peoples of central America.

Modern science is now beginning to unlock the mysterious and complex secrets of the cocoa bean, confirming what ancient man always believed. Far from being bad for your health, cocoa has been reinstated as a food which is beneficial in many ways.

Some research has even suggested that eating small amounts of chocolate could help you live longer, as long as it is low in fat and sugar and contains a high percentage of cocoa solids.

Once reserved for the elite of society and used in religious ritual, the last 150 years have seen chocolate become a part of everyday life.

Recently, however, the chocolate tree has been returning to its origins. Single estate, high-quality chocolate, flavoured with spices that even the Aztecs would recognise, is now available at the fashionable end of the market.